BLESSED PARADOXES
The Beatitudes as Painted Prayer

illustrated by
Dee Schenck Rhodes

text by
Barbara Cawthorne Crafton

Illustrations copyright © 1998 by Dee Schenck Rhodes
Text copyright © 1998 by Barbara Cawthorne Crafton

Morehouse Publishing
P.O. Box 1321
Harrisburg, PA 17105

Morehouse Publishing is a division of The Morehouse Group.

The Scripture quotations contained herein are from the New Revised
Standard Version Bible, copyright © 1998 by the Division of Christian
Education of the National Council of the Churches of Christ in the
U.S.A., 475 Riverside Drive, New York, NY 10115-0050.

Printed in Malaysia
Photograph of Barbara Cawthorne Crafton by Susan Lerner.
Cover design by Trude Brummer

Library of Congress Cataloging-in-Publication Data

Crafton, Barbara Cawthorne.
    Blessed paradoxes : the Beatitudes as painted prayer
/ illustrated by Dee Schenk Rhodes ; text by Barbara
Cawthorne Crafton.
      p.   cm.
    ISBN 0-8192-1763-8 (hardcover)
    1. Bible. N.T. Matthew V, 1–12—Poetry. 2. Bible.
N.T. Matthew V, 1–12—Illustrations. 3. Christian poetry,
American.
4. Beatitudes—Illustrations. 5. Beatitudes—Poetry. I. Title.
PS3553.R217B58 1998
811'.54—dc21   98–28299
                                                                          CIP

For my husband Mac,
who has given me a place, in every sense,
to live, to work, to love,

In memory of my father,
David Schenck
who let me invade his paints and brushes
and got me started on my way

And for all those who seek to turn the world upside-down,
saying that there is another King—
Jesus.

        —D.S.R.

To Bill Williams,
1960–1998
At rest, in vigorous peace

        —B.C.C.

CONTENTS

FOREWORD

The Jews, that singular, God-obsessed people who are neither a race nor a nation, have walked through human history for as many eons as history has been capable of recording itself. Perhaps, according to the sacred text, even for eons before the coming of such human literacy. But wherever they went and under whatever circumstances they lived, the Jews were Jews only in so far as they kept Torah. All things depended, as they still do, on one abiding encounter on Sinai when two tables of ten laws became identity and vocation as well as the stuff of a consuming absorption.

God Himself had opened time on that mountain. With the finger of one hand, He had pierced the dividing line between All and part, and with that finger had defined in human words the perfecting code of the creature. Wherever the Jew went after that moment of penetration, Torah went; and wherever Torah went, the Jew attended it. Through all the exigencies of dispossession and the glories of conquest, through triumph and near annihilation, there always was Torah, the proof of divine selection and the perfect statement of divine, unattainable expectation.

As for the Jew, so too for the Christian the Law still obtains, still holds sanctity of place as the sublimely given; for the Christian follows the God-sired Jew who taught us, saying, Do not imagine that I have come to abolish the Law and the Prophets. I have come not to abolish but to complete them." And who, lest there should ever be any question, then added, "I tell you solemnly, till heaven and earth disappear, not one dot, not one little stroke, shall disappear from the Law until its purpose is achieved."

Like the finger of His Father's hand on Sinai, this Jew too was a penetration into time by the divine, a piercing of the creature's existence by the Creator's affection. And in the hands of the Son, the ten parts of Torah were distilled into two commandments and extended by eight mysteries. "You must love the Lord your God with all your heart and with all your mind. This is the greatest and first commandment. The second resembles it: You must love your neighbor as yourself. On these two commandments hang the whole Law, and the Prophets also," were the distillation. "Blessed are the meek, the poor in spirit, the peacemakers, those who hunger after righteousness, and those who mourn. Blessed also are the merciful and the pure in heart and the persecuted," were the mysteries, for they both describe the Father's beloved and prescribe, by extension, the way of being that the beloved must enter into, the paradoxical way of being and of becoming that is the courtship of Christian devotion.

As the Jew and Judaism over the centuries have pondered Torah, have turned it from side to side, have considered it as one considers a perfectly polished orb, have studied in exquisite detail its every possibility, have even made it a kind of temple of the heart when only a remnant of a physical Temple was left to an exiled experience—in all these ways so too has the Christian engaged and reverenced the two commandments and eight blessings of the Galilean. Like the Jews, Christians have pondered with amazement the perfection of the ten together and then have been awe-filled all over again by their own amazement. And over the centuries we have created volume after volume of commentary and celebration that continue to instruct the Christian heart as well as inspire the Christian mind.

What you are about to enter here as you turn the page to begin this book is another such celebration… a celebration not of the Christ's two-part summation of the Law, but of His eight blessings that expand and define it. The work of the poet Barbara Cawthorne Crafton and the painter Dee Schenck Rhodes, the words and images that follow here, like the tradition out of which they come, are a temple of sorts, a housing for the words of God as incarnated by ecstatic and believing artists. To enter this temple is to enter the beating heart of holiness. As with all such entrances, let us go quietly and with purpose to know and serve the Lord.

— *Phyllis Tickle*

HOW TO PAINT A PARADOX

The sixteen paintings in this book were originally eight drawings that kept splitting in two. As I struggled to find images for each Beatitude, I found myself constantly dividing the paper into two sections. The two parts of each blessing wouldn't come together into one image. I began to see that the Beatitudes described two distinct Kingdoms, requiring a series of paired images depicting the Kingdom of the World and the Kingdom of Heaven. Objectively, the figures in the Kingdom of the World paintings occupy the same time and place as the figures in the Kingdom of Heaven paintings. But seen from God's perspective, they are in a completely different place. Thus the smaller black and white paintings depict the "right-side-up" world view of the Kingdom of the World, and the larger, full color paintings depict the "upside-down" world of the Kingdom of Heaven.

When we look at loss and the emptiness of life from a purely human perspective, we see the dark, small series. When we turn around and begin to see things from God's perspective, we see things in the full color of God's ultimate intention, an intention that is even now breaking into the world as we know it.

Each condition that is presented in the Beatitudes is blessed by being brought into the Kingdom of Heaven. If a condition such as "poor in spirit" were kept in objective reality, the idea of its leading to the inheritance of a kingdom would remain an impossibility, a nonsensical paradox. Yet once poverty of spirit is brought into the Kingdom of Heaven, the paradox melts away and the reality of its inheritance is made clear. By creating a double series of paintings instead of one, the paradoxical tensions are resolved, as the second series takes each condition to a higher plane. There, in the realm of God's grace through Christ, we are free to stand and know His blessing.

— Dee Schenck Rhodes

Blessed are the poor in spirit, for theirs
is the kingdom of heaven."

— Matthew 7:3

BLESSED ARE THE POOR IN SPIRIT

It wasn't that I did not know
about the poor. Of course I knew.
They are always in the paper.
They trudge out of town
with suitcases. They poke

through ruined houses, unearth
broken teacups, half a doll.
They are the next of kin;
they lift the corner of a sheet.
Of course I knew. I only didn't know

that I was one of them.
Please pardon me. I cannot rise.
I am poorer
than I thought. Fetal I, who curl,
protecting what remains

of my soft organs
with carapace of spine,
but make no refuge, nothing
from myself to help myself.
So this is poverty — it is so still.

Yet from its very scar,
a loving hand,
another's, not my own,
uncoils and lifts.

Blessed are those who mourn,
for they will be comforted."

— Matthew 7:4

BLESSED ARE

THOSE WHO

MOURN

It cannot be,
but is.
I cannot live
through this,
but do.
Bleached by grief, wail
my cry gnaws inward,
lodges in the throat, lives there
(my only guest).

Spirit, warm my exile,
mother me.
With your soft fire,
visit.

Blessed are the meek, for they
will inherit the earth."

— Matthew 7:5

BLESSED ARE
THE MEEK

It's only me,
unentitled
now, as always, and unsung,
nothing much of which
to sing. I yet expect,
know more now than I ever
knew before, of love that never
polls the crowd,
or honors place or pride.
Nothing
to commend me to you
but your love. And so
the world is mine, held lightly.
It is yours,
it and I and all in us,
all yours.

Blessed are those who hunger and thirst for righteousness, for they will be filled."

— Matthew 7:6

BLESSED ARE THOSE
WHO HUNGER
AND THIRST FOR
RIGHTEOUSNESS

I no longer clutch at things that are
not mine. I see that all is gift
and all is thine. A holier hunger
hollows me, a thirst for thee, a longing
to be godly, loving, free. To chafe at evil
as I used to fight my good, wanting
all the world to taste the food
of shared communion under heaven's roof.
I will not rest. Your love
will fuel my own.
And I will yearn until
the world is home.

B lessed are the merciful, for they
will receive mercy."

— Matthew 7:7

BLESSED ARE
THE MERCIFUL

My baby was hurt. She moaned away
drugged hours, arms bound (she might disturb
her dressing if her hands were free), pinioned,
cruciform, behind the metal bars,
and I beside. To touch or not to touch?
My touch reminded her of magic
mother power, my healing touch,
of finger and of knee,
that keeps all pain at bay. It didn't work
today. She cried the more.

Midnight. Nurses crept about
and in and out: Anything you need?
     No.
     Well, yes —
     No.
     Thank you.

And then, a friend, a mother, older one
than I, came to stand beside
and with a soft hand stroked
my hair, brought oatmeal
in a thermos, hot taste of a morning
that would come.
Then, leaving it in pledge
we all would wake,
she went on home.

Blessed are the pure in heart,
for they will see God."

— Matthew 7:8

BLESSED
ARE THE PURE
IN HEART

The heart: manifestly not sinless,
has ventricles, heart-wombs,
made to receive.
Faithful it beats, coaxes darkened blood
toward its brightening.
This is purification; without it we die.

Seat of faith, for Doctors of the Church
and modern publicists,
tied to feeling of which it knows nothing,
battered, without and within,
by its own hand and by the hands of others,
shocked by sudden loss, by fear,
sometimes even killed,
dead from fear of dying.

A new heart.
Aware that it will end, content
to have it so. A center unfocused
and undivided:
this is not natural.
Such a heart is schooled.

Blessed are the peacemakers, for they will
be called children of God."

— Matthew 7:9

BLESSED ARE THE PEACEMAKERS

This is not war, and yet it is
not peace. The worried in-laws phone:
"It may be too much work, or too few
children. Too much money?
Insufficient funds?
And yet, I'm sure they'll come
around. We had rough sledding
once, you will recall,
and we came out all right."

But lasting strangeness daily seems
more sane, acquires a coat of reason,
some new ease. It now seems
no great matter, their own affair
and no one else's business.
Philosophic rightness welds to it:
they now remember ancient
slights as yesterday,
more weighty now than when they
first occurred. It now seems
they were never true or lovely—
how could they both have been
such fools? It now seems
quite a harmless thing
to leave, the common weal will not
be rent in twain, and any pain incurred
will be an Opportunity.

In careful cups of coffee
sipped in public, Solomonic puzzles
civilly discussed: there are some things
to be divided—some records
neither plays, but each desires,
the wedding china, and the kids.
Bricks of a history
laid together, a blood supply
not fully understood: first timid forays
into common ground.

"This might be dangerous."
"Might be amputation after all."

Can we find work again for love
in this sad space? Can homely face
and homely clothing in the closet
again betoken heart and mind?
Can more than fear cement us?
And add our home to earthly
sum of peace?

Blessed are those who are persecuted
for righteousness' sake, for theirs is
the kingdom of heaven."

— Matthew 7:10

BLESSED ARE

THOSE WHO ARE

PERSECUTED FOR

RIGHTEOUSNESS' SAKE

These are those who washed their robes
in blood. Their own, the Lamb's,
commingle. For them we fashion
diadems of myth, sew coats of scruple
never worn in life;
they neither wear them now.
If roses spring up from their graves
or miracles embroider their biographies,
these add no needed beauty. The love of God
was love enough for them:

righteous more than innocent.
    (Those two sleep in different beds,
      and shop in different stores.)
There was more to their goodness
than avoidance, than staying
clean a life, and dying clean.
They paid a dearer price, and chose to pay,
the choice a gift.
These, though maculate,
are cleansed. They

shine
like Moses,
shine
like Christ,
shine
like God,

give back glory.

DEE SCHENCK RHODES was born in Greensboro, North Carolina, and received classical training in drawing and painting while attending high school. She focused on music in college and graduate school, but returned to the visual arts gradually, exploring watercolors, printmaking, and hand-built ceramics. Her primary medium, though, continues to be oil painting. She lives with her family in South Carolina.

BARBARA CAWTHORNE CRAFTON, an Episcopal priest, currently serves as rector of St. Clement's Church in Manhattan's theater district. She is the author of *The Sewing Room: Uncommon Reflections on Life, Love and Work, Meditations on the Book of Psalms* and others.